CELEBRATIONS

CELEBRATIONS

MAYA ANGELOU

Rituals of Peace and Prayer

virago

VIRAGO

First published in Great Britain in 2007 by Virago Press
First published in the United States in 2006 by Random House

Copyright © 2006 Maya Angelou

The moral right of the author has been asserted.

*All characters and events in this publication, other than those
clearly in the public domain, are fictitious and any resemblance
to real persons, living or dead, is purely coincidental.*

The following poems have been previously published:
'On the Pulse of Morning', 'A Brave and Startling Truth',
'When Great Trees Fall', 'Amazing Peace', and 'Mother'.

A CIP catalogue record for this book
is available from the British Library.

ISBN 978-1-84408-465-4

Typeset in Fournier by M Rules
Printed and bound in Great Britain by
Clays Ltd, St Ives plc

Virago Press
An imprint of
Little, Brown Book Group
100 Victoria Embankment
London EC4Y 0DY

An Hachette Livre UK Company

www.virago.co.uk

DEDICATED TO

Brandon Bailey Johnson

Caylin Nicole Johnson

Elliott Jones

Lydia Stuckey

CONTENTS

ON THE PULSE
OF MORNING

We had a lesson at

SHAKESPEARE'S
SCHOOLROOM
& GUILDHALL

A Rock, a River, a Tree,

Hosts to species long since departed,

Marked the mastodon.

The dinosaur, who left dry tokens

Of their sojourn here

On our planet floor.

Any broad alarm of their hastening doom

Is lost in the gloom of dust and ages.

But today, the Rock cries out to us, clearly,

forcefully,

Come, you may stand upon my back

And face your distant destiny,

But seek no haven in my shadow.

I will give you no hiding place down here.

You, created only a little lower than

The angels, have crouched too long in

The bruising darkness,

Have lain too long

Face down in ignorance,

Your mouths spilling words

Armed for slaughter.

The Rock cries out today, you may stand

     on me,

But do not hide your face.

Across the wall of the world,

A River sings a beautiful song,

Come rest here by my side.

Each of you a bordered country,

Delicate and strangely made, proud,

Yet thrusting perpetually under siege.

Your armed struggles for profit

Have left collars of waste upon

My shore, currents of debris upon my breast.

Yet, today I call you to my riverside,

If you will study war no more. Come,

Clad in peace, and I will sing the songs

The Creator gave to me when I and the

Tree and the stone were one.

Before cynicism was a bloody sear across your

Brow and when you yet knew you still

Knew nothing.

The River sings and sings on.

There is a true yearning to respond to

The singing River and the wise Rock.

So say the Asian, the Hispanic, the Jew,

The African and Native American, the Sioux,

The Catholic, the Muslim, the French,

    the Greek,

The Irish, the Rabbi, the Priest, the Sheikh,

The Gay, the Straight, the Preacher,

The Privileged, the Homeless, the Teacher.

They hear. They all hear

The speaking of the Tree.

Today, the first and last of every Tree

Speaks to humankind. Come to me, here

    beside the River.

Plant yourself beside me, here beside

    the River.

Each of you, descendant of some

Passed-on traveler, has been paid for.

You who gave me my first name, you

Pawnee, Apache, and Seneca, you

Cherokee Nation, who rested with me, then,

Forced on bloody feet, left me to the

    employment of

Other seekers — desperate for gain,

Starving for gold.

You the Turk, the Swede, the German,

 the Italian, the Scot,

You the Ashanti, the Yoruba, the Kru,

 bought,

Sold, stolen, arriving on a nightmare,

Praying for a dream.

Here, root yourselves beside me.

I am the Tree planted by the River,

Which will not be moved.

I the Rock, I the River, I the Tree

I am yours — your Passages have been paid.

Lift up your faces, you have a piercing need

For this bright morning dawning for you.

History, despite its wrenching pain,

Cannot be unlived, and if faced

With courage, need not be lived again.

Lift up your eyes upon

The day breaking for you.

Give birth again

To the dream.

Women, children, men,

Take it into the palms of your hands.

Mold it into the shape of your most

Private need. Sculpt it into

The image of your most public self.

Lift up your hearts.

Each new hour holds new chances

For new beginnings.

Do not be wedded forever

To fear, yoked eternally

To brutishness.

The horizon leans forward,

Offering you space to place new steps of

    change.

Here, on the pulse of this fine day,

You may have the courage

To look up and out upon me, the

Rock, the River, the Tree, your country.

No less to Midas than the mendicant.

No less to you now than the mastodon then.

Here on the pulse of this new day

You may have the grace to look up, and out

And into your sister's eyes, into

Your brother's face, your country,

And say simply,

Very simply,

With hope,

Good morning.

A BRAVE AND
STARTLING TRUTH

Dedicated to the hope for peace, which lies,

sometimes hidden, in every heart.

We, this people, on a small and lonely planet

Traveling through casual space

Past aloof stars, across the way of indifferent

    suns

To a destination where all signs tell us

It is possible and imperative that we learn

A brave and startling truth.

And when we come to it

To the day of peacemaking

When we release our fingers

From fists of hostility

When we come to it

When the curtain falls on the minstrel show

of hate

And faces sooted with scorn are scrubbed

clean

When battlefields and coliseum

No longer rake our unique and particular

sons and daughters

Up with the bruised and bloody grass

To lay them in identical plots in foreign soil

When the rapacious storming of the churches

The screaming racket in the temples have

ceased

When the pennants are waving gaily

When the banners of the world tremble

Stoutly in a good, clean breeze

When we come to it

When we let the rifles fall from our shoulders

And our children can dress their dolls in flags

    of truce

When land mines of death have been removed

And the aged can walk into evenings of peace

When religious ritual is not perfumed

By the incense of burning flesh

And childhood dreams are not kicked awake

By nightmares of sexual abuse

When we come to it

Then we will confess that not the Pyramids

With their stones set in mysterious perfection

Nor the Gardens of Babylon

Hanging as eternal beauty

In our collective memory

Not the Grand Canyon

Kindled into delicious color

By Western sunsets

Nor the Danube, flowing its blue soul into

    Europe

Not the sacred peak of Mount Fuji

Stretching to the Rising Sun

Neither Father Amazon nor Mother

    Mississippi

    who, without favor,

Nurtures all creatures in their depths and on

    their shores

These are not the only wonders of

    the world

When we come to it

We, this people, on this minuscule globe

Who reach daily for the bomb, the blade,

    and the dagger

Yet who petition in the dark for tokens of

    peace

We, this people, on this mote of matter

In whose mouths abide cankerous words

Which challenge our very existence

Yet out of those same mouths

Can come songs of such exquisite sweetness

That the heart falters in its labor

And the body is quieted into awe

We, this people, on this small and drifting

    planet

Whose hands can strike with such abandon

That, in a twinkling, life is sapped from the

living

Yet those same hands can touch with such

healing,

irresistible tenderness,

That the haughty neck is happy to bow

And the proud back is glad to bend

Out of such chaos, of such contradiction

We learn that we are neither devils nor

divines

When we come to it

We, this people, on this wayward, floating

body

Created on this earth, of this earth

Have the power to fashion for this earth

A climate where every man and every woman

Can live freely without sanctimonious piety

Without crippling fear

When we come to it

We must confess that we are the possible

We are the miraculous, we are the true

      wonder of this world

That is when, and only when,

We come to it.

CONTINUE

Dear Oprah,

On the day of your birth

The Creator filled countless storehouses and

    stockings

With rich ointments

Luscious tapestries

And antique coins of incredible value

Jewels worthy of a queen's dowry

They were set aside for your use

Alone

Armed with faith and hope

And without knowing of the wealth which

    awaited

You broke through dense walls

Of poverty

And loosed the chains of ignorance which

    threatened to cripple you so that you

    could walk

A free woman

Into a world which needed you

My wish for you

Is that you continue

Continue

To be who and how you are

To astonish a mean world

With your acts of kindness

Continue

To allow humor to lighten the burden

Of your tender heart

Continue

In a society dark with cruelty

To let the people hear the grandeur

Of God in the peals of your laughter

Continue

To let your eloquence

Elevate the people to heights

They had only imagined

Continue

To remind the people that

Each is as good as the other

And that no one is beneath

Nor above you

Continue

To remember your own young years

And look with favor upon the lost

And the least and the lonely

Continue

To put the mantel of your protection

Around the bodies of

The young and defenseless

Continue

To take the hand of the despised

And diseased and walk proudly with them

In the high street

Some might see you and

Be encouraged to do likewise

Continue

To plant a public kiss of concern

On the cheek of the sick

And the aged and infirm

And count that as a

Natural action to be expected

Continue

To let gratitude be the pillow

Upon which you kneel to

Say your nightly prayer

And let faith be the bridge

You build to overcome evil

And welcome good

Continue

To ignore no vision

Which comes to enlarge your range

And increase your spirit

Continue

To dare to love deeply

And risk everything

For the good thing

Continue

To float

Happily in the sea of infinite substance

Which set aside riches for you

Before you had a name

Continue

And by doing so

You and your work

Will be able to continue

    Eternally

        HAPPY BIRTHDAY!

SONS AND
DAUGHTERS

If my luck is bad

And his aim is straight

I will leave my life

On the killing field

You can see me die

On the nightly news

As you settle down

To your evening meal.

But you'll turn your back

As you often do

Yet I am your sons

And your daughters too.

In the city streets

Where the neon lights

Turn my skin from black

To electric blue

My hope soaks red

On the gray pavement

And my dreams die hard

For my life is through.

But you'll turn your back

As you often do

Yet I am your sons

And your daughters too.

In the little towns

Of this mighty land

Where you close your eyes

To my crying need

I strike out wild

And my brother falls

Turn on your news

You can watch us bleed.

In morgues I'm known

By a numbered tag

In clinics and jails

And junkyards too

You deny my kin

Though I bear your name

For I am a part

Of mankind too.

But you'll turn your back

As you often do

Yet I am your sons

And your daughters too.

Turn your face to me

Please

Let your eyes seek my eyes

Lay your hand upon my arm

Touch me. I am real as flesh

And solid as bone.

I am no metaphor

I am no symbol

I am not a nightmare

To vanish with the dawn

I am lasting as hunger

And certain as midnight.

I claim that no council nor committee

Can contain me

Nor fashion me to its whim.

You, come here, hunch with me in this dingy

     doorway,

Face with me the twisted mouth threat

Of one more desperate

And better armed than I.

Join me again at today's dime store counter

Where the word to me

Is still no.

Let us go, your shoulder,

Against my shoulder,

To the new picket line

Where my color is still a signal

For brutes to spew their bile

Like spit in my eye.

You, only you, who have made me

Who share this tender taunting history

    with me

My fathers and mothers

Only you can save me

Only you can order the tides,

That rush my heart, to cease

Stop expanding my veins

Into red riverlets.

Come, you my relative

Walk the forest floor with me

Where rampaging animals lurk,

Lusting for my future

Only if your side is by my side

Only if your side is by my side

Will I survive.

But you'll probably turn your back

As you often do

Yet I am your sons

And your daughters too.

WHEN GREAT
TREES FALL

Dedicated to Bernice Johnson Reegon

of Sweet Honey in the Rock

When great trees fall,

rocks on distant hills shudder,

lions hunker down

in tall grasses,

and even elephants

lumber after safety.

When great trees fall

in forests,

small things recoil into silence,

their senses

eroded beyond fear.

When great souls die,

the air around us becomes

light, rare, sterile.

We breathe briefly.

Our eyes, briefly,

see with

a hurtful clarity.

Our memory, suddenly sharpened,

examines,

gnaws on kind words

unsaid,

promised walks

never taken.

Great souls die and

our reality, bound to

them, takes leave of us.

Our souls,

dependent upon their

nurture,

now shrink, wizened.

Our minds, formed

and informed by their

radiance,

fall away.

We are not so much maddened

as reduced to the unutterable ignorance

of dark, cold

caves.

And when great souls die,

after a period peace blooms,

slowly and always

irregularly. Spaces fill

with a kind of

soothing electric vibration.

Our senses, restored, never

to be the same, whisper to us,

They existed. They existed.

We can be. Be and be

better. For they existed.

A BLACK WOMAN
SPEAKS TO
BLACK MANHOOD

Our souls look back

In wondrous surprise

At how we have made it

So far from where we started

Fathers, brothers, uncles

Nephews, sons, and friends

Look over your shoulders

And at our history

The night was long

The wounds were deep

The pit has been dark

Its walls were steep

I was dragged by braids

On a sandy beach

I was pulled near you

But beyond your reach

You were bound and gagged

When you heard me cry

Your spirit was wounded

With each wrenching try

For you thrusted and pulled

Trying to break free

So that neither of us

Would know slavery

You forgot the strength

Of the rope and the chain

You only remember

Your manhood shame

You couldn't help yourself

And you couldn't help me

You've carried that fact

Down our history

We have survived

Those centuries of hate

And we do not deny

Their bruising weight

Please my many million men

Let us lay that image aside

See how our people today

Walk in strength and in pride

Celebrate, stand up, clap hands for ourselves

     and those who went before

Stand up, clap hands, let us welcome kind

     words back into our vocabulary

Stand up, clap hands, let us welcome

     courtesies back into our bedrooms

Stand up, clap hands, let us invite generosity

  back into our kitchens

Clap hands, let faith find a place in

  our souls

Clap hands, let hope live in our hearts

We have survived

And even thrived with

Passion

Compassion

Humor

and style

The night was long

The wounds were deep

The pit was dark

Its walls were steep

Clap hands, celebrate

We deserve it

Jubilate!

AMAZING PEACE

Thunder rumbles in the mountain passes
And lightning rattles the eaves of our houses.
Floodwaters await in our avenues.

Snow falls upon snow, falls upon snow
            to avalanche
Over unprotected villages.
The sky slips low and gray and threatening.

We question ourselves. What have we done to
            so affront nature?
We interrogate and worry God.

Are you there? Are you there, really?

Does the covenant you made with us still

    hold?

Into this climate of fear and apprehension,

    Christmas enters,

Streaming lights of joy, ringing bells of hope

And singing carols of forgiveness high up in

    the bright air.

The world is encouraged to come away from

    rancor,

Come the way of friendship.

It is the Glad Season.

Thunder ebbs to silence and lightning sleeps

    quietly in the corner.

Floodwaters recede into memory.

Snow becomes a yielding cushion to aid us

As we make our way to higher ground.

Hope is born again in the faces of children.

It rides on the shoulders of our aged as they

    walk into their sunsets.

Hope spreads around the earth, brightening

    all things,

Even hate, which crouches breeding in dark

    corridors.

In our joy, we think we hear a whisper.

At first it is too soft. Then only half heard.

We listen carefully as it gathers strength.

We hear a sweetness.

The word is Peace.

It is loud now.

Louder than the explosion of bombs.

We tremble at the sound. We are thrilled by
    its presence.

It is that for which we have hungered.

Not just the absence of war. But true Peace.

A harmony of spirit, a comfort of courtesies.

Security for our beloveds and their beloveds.

We clap hands and welcome the Peace of
    Christmas.

We beckon this good season to wait awhile
    with us.

We, Baptist and Buddhist, Methodist and
    Muslim, say come.

Peace.

Come and fill us and our world with your
    majesty.

We, the Jew and the Jainist, the Catholic and
    the Confucian,

Implore you to stay awhile with us

So we may learn by your shimmering light

How to look beyond complexion and see
    community.

It is Christmas time, a halting of hate time.

On this platform of peace, we can create a
    language

To translate ourselves to ourselves and to

each other.

At this Holy Instant, we celebrate the Birth of

Jesus Christ

Into the great religions of the world.

We jubilate the precious advent of trust.

We shout with glorious tongues the coming of

hope.

All the earth's tribes loosen their voices

To celebrate the promise of Peace.

We, Angels and Mortals, Believers and

Nonbelievers,

Look heavenward and speak the word aloud.

Peace. We look at our world and speak the

word aloud.

Peace. We look at each other, then into

ourselves,

And we say without shyness or apology or

hesitation:

Peace, My Brother.

Peace, My Sister.

Peace, My Soul.

MOTHER

A Cradle to Hold Me

It is true

I was created in you.

It is also true

That you were created for me.

I owned your voice.

It was shaped and tuned to soothe me.

Your arms were molded

Into a cradle to hold me, to rock me.

The scent of your body was the air

Perfumed for me to breathe.

Mother,

During those early, dearest days

I did not dream that you had

A larger life which included me,

Among your other concerns,

For I had a life

Which was only you.

Time passed steadily and drew us apart.

I was unwilling.

I feared if I let you go

You would leave me eternally.

You smiled at my fears, saying

I could not stay in your lap forever

That one day you would have to stand

And where would I be?

You smiled again.

I did not.

Without warning you left me,

But you returned immediately.

You left again and returned,

I admit, quickly.

But relief did not rest with me easily.

You left again, but again returned.

You left again, but again returned.

Each time you reentered my world

You brought assurance.

Slowly I gained confidence.

You thought you knew me,

But I did know you,

You thought you were watching me,

But I did hold you securely in my sight,

Recording every movement,

Memorizing your smiles, tracing your frowns.

In your absence

I rehearsed you,

The way you had of singing

On a breeze,

While a sob lay

At the root of your song.

The way you posed your head

So that the light could caress your face

When you put your fingers on my hand

And your hand on my arm,

I was blessed with a sense of health,

Of strength and very good fortune.

You were always

The heart of happiness to me,

Bringing nougats of glee,

Sweets of open laughter.

I loved you even during the years

When you knew nothing

And I knew everything, I loved you still.

Condescendingly of course,

From my high perch

Of teenage wisdom.

I spoke sharply to you, often

Because you were slow to understand.

I grew older and

Was stunned to find

How much knowledge you had gleaned.

And so quickly.

Mother, I have learned enough now

To know I have learned nearly nothing.

On this day

When mothers are being honored,

Let me thank you

That my selfishness, ignorance, and mockery

Did not bring you to

Discard me like a broken doll

Which had lost its favor.

I thank you that

You still find something in me

To cherish, to admire, and to love.

I thank you, Mother.

I love you.

IN AND OUT
OF TIME

For Jessica and Colin Johnson

Stephanie and Guy Johnson

The sun has come out

The mists have gone

We see in the distance

Our long way home

I was yours to love

You were always mine

We have belonged together

In and out of time

When the first stone looked

Up at the blazing sun

And the first tree struggled

From the forest floor

I loved you more

You were the rhythm on the head

Of the conga drum

And the brush of palm

On my nut brown skin

And I loved you then

We worked the cane

And cotton fields

We trod together

The city streets

Wearied by labor

Bruised by cruelty

Strutting and sassy

To our inner beat

And all the while

Lord, how I love your smile

You've freed your braids

Gave your hair to the breeze

It hummed like a hive

Of busy bees

I reached into the mass

For the honeycomb there

God, how I loved your hair

You saw me bludgeoned

By circumstance

Injured by hate

And lost to chance

Legs that could be broken

But knees that would not bend

Oh, you loved me then

I raked the Heavens' belly

With torrid screams

I fought to turn

Nightmares into dreams

My protests were loud

And brash and bold

My, how you loved my soul

The sun has come out

The mists have gone

We see in the distance

Our long way home

I was yours to love

And you were always mine

We have belonged together

In and out of time

BEN LEAR'S
BAR MITZVAH

AN ODE TO BEN LEAR

ON THE OCCASION OF HIS BAR MITZVAH

To you

in your walled city of childhood,

the years have inched by slowly, tortoise-like

crawling,

yet to your family and family of friends

the time has hurried, without halting,

without leaving enough seasons in which

to know you, to teach you, to love you.

You have been noted studying the Torah,

probing the words of ancient prophets

reading,

To many

you have come too suddenly to the new

region of manhood.

To your parents,

in whose immense realm of love

you have been clasped and claimed,

you are still the tender-tough boy,

yet in your face, they see already the promise

of the man you are becoming.

To them

you are too eager to step into the new land,

too ready to share the responsibility

with the citizens of your new country.

Some of your beloveds

are longing to hold you back in the safe arms

of childhood,

where errant behavior could meet with soft

admonishment,

where most injuries could be made better by

a mother's kiss,

but even now you are leaning away toward

the horizon

with one foot raised to step forward.

None can stop you, none can stay you.

Please know,

prayers lay in the road where you will plant

your feet.

Please know

that aspirations of your family are high at

    your back, and surround you entirely.

Please know

that great hopes of your devoted shower

    you with

ardent wishes for your being and for your

    future.

Your beloveds

know that you are entering a nation

where you must learn the difference

between seeking after justice

and lusting for revenge.

They know also

that you will meet those who would be kind

if only they had the courage, and

those who would do evil

if only they had the opportunity.

You will be bathed in the morning dew of

    truth

and you will drink down the brackish water of

    false witness.

Be wary, my nephew, but fear only God,

for you have a limitless resource of powerful

    love

to evoke and call forth

and I,

prompt with all your primed and loving

    family,

await your summons.

VIGIL

For Luther Vandross and Barry White

We are born in pain, then relief comes.

We are lost in the dark, then day breaks.

We are confused, confounded, and fearful,

Then faith takes our hand.

We stumble and fumble and fall,

Then, we rise.

Into each of our meanest nights, you

      have arrived,

Oh, Lord,

Creator,

To lead us away from our ignorance

And into knowing.

Now, we gather at your altar,

Rich and poor, young and

Achingly old,

We are the housed and the homeless,

We are the lucky,

And the lazy.

As if at the foot

Of an ancient baobab tree,

In this moment

We gather to stand, kneel, sit, squat, and

    crumple here,

Knowing that, when the medical geniuses

Have done their best,

When the Nobel Prize Winners

Have used their most powerful energy,

We have You.

Creator,

We bring to You

Our brothers, sons, fathers, uncles,

Nephews, cousins, beloved, and friends.

We place the body of Luther Vandross

And the body of Barry White

Here before You.

They are among the best we have

And You are all we have.

Heal, we pray.

Heal, we pray.

Heal us all,

We pray.

PRAYER

Father Mother God, thank You for Your

presence during the hard and mean days.

For then we have You to lean upon.

Thank You for Your presence during the

bright and sunny days, for then we can

share that which we have with those who have less.

And thank You for Your presence during the

Holy Days, for then we are able to

celebrate You and our families and our
friends.

For those who have no voice, we ask You
to speak.

For those who feel unworthy, we ask You
to pour Your love out in waterfalls of
tenderness.

For those who live in pain, we ask You to
bathe them in the river of Your healing.

For those who are lonely, we ask You to keep
them company.

For those who are depressed, we ask You to

shower upon them the light of hope.

Dear Creator, You, the borderless sea of

substance, we ask You to give to all the

world that which we need most – Peace.

Amen.